6/24 GA698 1·00

GW01417833

A HOME FOR DOG

by Barbara Mitchelhill

pictures by
Barbara Walker

Tom, Mum and Grandad had just moved
to a big, old house . . .

with a big, old garden.

'Wouldn't it be good to have a dog here,' said Tom.
'Yes,' said Grandad, 'but how would we look after it?'

4

'I could feed it,'
said Mum.

5

'And I could brush it every day,'
said Tom.

6

'And I could take it for walks,'
said Grandad.

7

So, they got everything ready for a dog.
First, they made a bed for it to sleep in . . .

then they bought bowls and some food . . . .

10   and then they bought a collar and a lead.

'Now we're ready for a dog,' said Tom.

So, they went on a bus to the other side of town.

'This is where we'll find a dog,' said Mum.

13

There were lots of dogs there . . .

and they all needed a home.
It was hard to choose.

But at last they chose Katy.